Magdalena Natalia Zalewski

Earth Day, a Story of Success

**Progresses and Backstrokes of American Environmentalism During the
Last Forty Years**

GRIN Verlag

Bibliografische Information der Deutschen Nationalbibliothek:

Die Deutsche Bibliothek verzeichnet diese Publikation in der Deutschen National-
bibliografie; detaillierte bibliografische Daten sind im Internet über http://dnb.d-
nb.de/ abrufbar.

Impressum:

Copyright © 2010 GRIN Verlag, Open Publishing GmbH
Druck und Bindung: Books on Demand GmbH, Norderstedt Germany
ISBN: 978-3-640-82993-4

Dieses Buch bei GRIN:

http://www.grin.com/de/e-book/166641/earth-day-a-story-of-success

GRIN - Your knowledge has value

Der GRIN Verlag publiziert seit 1998 wissenschaftliche Arbeiten von Studenten, Hochschullehrern und anderen Akademikern als eBook und gedrucktes Buch. Die Verlagswebsite www.grin.com ist die ideale Plattform zur Veröffentlichung von Hausarbeiten, Abschlussarbeiten, wissenschaftlichen Aufsätzen, Dissertationen und Fachbüchern.

Besuchen Sie uns im Internet:

http://www.grin.com/

http://www.facebook.com/grincom

http://www.twitter.com/grin_com

Earth Day, a Story of Success: Progresses and Backstrokes of American Environmentalism During the Last Forty Years

Term Paper: Summer Semester 2010
Deadline:October 30, 2010

Name: Magdalena Natalia Zalewski
Subject: American Cultural History
Course: American Environmental History

Table of Contents

1.Introductionp.3

2. American Environmentalism Now and Thenp.4

2.1. Earth Day, a Groundbreaking Idea p.4

2.2. Environmental Law and the US Government p.5

2.3. Ecological Consciousness or Ecofascism? p.7

3. Cures for the Cancer or Cancer for the Cure?p.9

3.1. Big Business and Economic Growth p.9

3.2. Technology and Science, A Solution For All Problems? p.11

4. The Third World and American Overpopulationp.13

5. Environmentally Friendly Behavior, a Question of Attitude?p.14

5.1. A Matter of Religion and Philosophy p.14

5.2. Environmental Education p.16

6. Conclusionp.17

7. Pictorial Sources p.19

8. Bibliography p. 22

1. Introduction

Everybody has heard of Earth Day at least once in a lifetime.Earth Day has been celebrated for the first time on April 22, 1970 in the whole United States.It was the largest demonstration that should ever take place in this country. Twenty million people, from coast to coast, gathered in cities around the nation to speak up for nature and to make environmentalism a political issue.

Today Earth Day is solemnized in over 175 countries around the globe; some local communities even dedicate themselves to the environmental good throughout a longer period, in a so-calledEarth Week or Earth Month around April 22.This year Earth Day has celebrated its 40th anniversary, but what has changed within these four decades? Did Earth Day and the idea behind it accomplish its goals, is the job to remedy the circumstance of our environment done or did it fail?Which environmental challenges did people face in the 1970s and which challenges do we face today? These questions are not easily answered.

The founder of Earth Day, Gaylord Nelson had the ideology to inspire awareness and appreciation for the earth's natural environment among people. It is sure that Nelson did not invent environmentalism; the environmental movement had its precursor in the conservation movement. Especially considering that ecologists like Aldo Leopold or Rachel Carson had set the benchmark for ecology and environmentalism with their literature earlier.

Nevertheless, Senator Gaylord Nelson was the first politician who realizedthat environmentalism was the most urgent task of the 20th century. It is a fact that environmentalism gained credence at the dawn of the 1970s environmentalism was no longer ignored, but fully respected by public, media and policy. Since then the U.S.Congress passed over thirty environmental laws and established offices, but is plain legislation enough?

"Think Globally. Act Locally." has been the Earth Day motto ever since, but indeed it is hard tomanage to live this way, to act locally for earth's and nature's sake.Undeniably, it is important to transform our society into a sustainable society, but first of all it is crucial to understand the structure of consumption in the Western world, especially the US.A lot of changes will be necessary to strike a new path for environmentalism, for true and deep ecology.

There are direct consequences for human intervention into ecosystems and they actually will drop back to humanity, if they have not already; but these ecological interplays are very complex, sensitive and hard to explain.

However, what seems to be most important is that every part of the society will play its role in the development of the ecological future.Involved parts throughout this process will be media, the public, environmental organizations, the government and enterprises.

Cooperation between each and everyone will be essential and above all environmental education will have to start in early infancy.Notably our success will depend on an interdisciplinary way of solving the environmental problem of today. To analyze the success of environmental progress and Earth Day in the United States of America, it is needful to collect historical, scientific, economic and philosophical information. Analysis is a guideline for behavioral change and problem solution.

Therefore which expectations did the people have for Earth Day, which promises were kept and broken within the last forty years?

To find answers as precise as possible I will especially focus on Earth Day agendas and essays around Earth Day and environmentalism to compare different opinions and ideas, written with various approaches by authors with different backgrounds. The spectrum will reach from ecologists, philosophers to economists, and chiefly be complemented with reference to the founder of Earth Day himself: Gaylord Nelson.

2. American Environmentalism Now and Then

It is obvious that since 1970 people have changed their minds to change the planet or at least they have realized that environmental pollution is hazardous to ecosystems, to the maintenance of species and to human health. But the question is, what caused these changes in specific, what has improved the environmental situation, and in contrast what endeavors failed and why? How far did legislation play a part in contributing to enhance the ecological situation? Why do people give Earth Day the leading role in the environmental movement and – investigating beyond the surface - are environmental organizations as immaculate as they appear?

2.1. Earth Day, a Groundbreaking Idea

In 1969theCuyahoga River burned, city smog was present everywhere, as other environmental catastrophes and ecological disasters hit the American nation between the 1940s and 1970s one by one.[1]Rachel Carson's non-fiction bookSilent Springpublished in 1962, a national bestseller, revealed the danger of pesticides, especially DDT, which lead for example to the extinction of the eastern anatum peregrine falcon.[2]During this period people's concern about the environment and pollution was silently growing.

Democrat Gaylord Nelson, who became senator of Wisconsin in 1962, recognized the problem. He knew that environmentalism had to become an important political issue.

Nelson had the idea that a national conservation tour, with president John F. Kennedy contributing speeches, could attract public attention. Kennedy supported this plan and so he, Nelson and several other senators did the conservation speaking tour in 1963, traveling eleven states in five days.The tour turned out to be quitedisappointing, it seemed as if press and public did not consider the environmental situation as threatening as the foreign policy of Cold War.[3]

For the next six years Nelson was struggling to arouse the public and government's interest in the environment, until he finally found his inspiration in the Summer of '69. It was not hard to realize that anti-Vietnam War demonstrations having spread around national campuses, made a great stir in public.If this anti-war movement was able to awaken society, why should not an environmental "teach-in" do so?

On September 20, 1969 Nelson proposed his idea of an environmental teach-in in front of a yet minor, but emergent conservation group in Seattle, WA.Earth Day seemed to organize itself; it was an idea that set public afire and managed to become a movement imposing new standards.

When April 22, 1970 became the appointed date for Earth Day, conservatives felt threatened by the upcoming dawn of ecology. Right-wing politicians even accused Nelson and his proponents of creating a communist conspiracy, for evidence they pointed out that April 22 was Vladimir Lenin's birthday. So was this new movement really treacherously communistic or was it rather highly democratic? Actually April 22 was chosen, because it was before school summer vacation and beyond college exam time.[4]

---

[1] Gaylord Nelson with Susan Campbell and Paul Wozniak, Beyond Earth Day: Fulfilling the Promise (The University of Wisconsin Press, 2002), p. 6

[2] William Leiss, "POLITICAL ASPECTS OF ENVIRONMENTAL ISSUES," ECOLOGICAL CONSCIOUSNESS: Essays from the Earthday X Colloqium ed. Robert C. Schultz, J. Donald Hughes (University Press of America, Inc., 1981), p. 246f.

[3] Board of Regents of the University of Wisconsin System Nelson Institute for Environmental Studies, Earth Day: a simple idea, a world of change, http://www.nelsonearthday.net/nelson/earthdayidea.htm (September 2010)

[4] Nelson, Beyond Earth Day: Fulfilling the Promise, p. 7f.

In February 1970, two months before Earth Day was held, the business magazine *Fortune* dedicated its entire fortieth anniversary release to "The Environment: A National Mission for the Seventies."*Fortune's* editors wrote that "Environmental anxieties have coalesced [into] a permanent part of the American awareness, part of the set of beliefs, values and goals within which U.S. business operates." and that conservation organizations, as the *Sierra Club* for example, were fighting a new environmental battle, supported by ardent lawyers.[5]

Necessary preparations for the first Earth Day got going, but the fact that private donors supported it, as Larry Rockefeller and labor unions cannot be suppressed, financial help was essential.[6]

All in all Earth Day appeared to be what people wanted and needed, otherwise twenty million American citizens would not have pooled together to demonstrate in the name of nature.

On April 22, 1970 a powerful public interest group emerged that politicians finally did not underestimate.

Earth Day was successful indeed and soon it was called the first D-Day of the environmental movement. It appeared as if public fell into euphoria. The *New York Times* described this phenomenon as a grassroots power that was able to exceed political boundaries. It did not matter, if someone was independent, left- or right- wing; Earth Day had its supporters everywhere.[7]Years before, only civil liberties campaigners, mostly participants of the civil rights and anti-war movement, had supported ecology; but after April 1970 environmentalism was not just an activists' concern anymore.

2.2. Environmental Law and the US Government

So what happened after Nelson's movement took the U.S. by storm? Whenever people preach Earth Day's success, they usually rely on a heavy list of federal environmental measures that have been adopted since 1970. That is an absolutely true fact, but a lot of environmentalists claim that environmental law began as a legacy of Earth Day, which is partly wrong. [8]

Environmental law already had a history of about twenty-five years back then, it occurred around 1945. Unfortunately it occurred in"the Pacific Northwest and on the High Plains during World War II the national state used law to impress nature into military service".[9]

Despite heavy governmental mistakes like that,congress did a few good jobs. The Federal Water Pollution Control Act (FWPCA) of 1972 for example, which was meant to protect interstate water quality, was altered five times before and already had its first appearance in 1948.[10] It was an inevitable law to protect citizens and nature, because states and cities were unable to solve or manage the problems they had with fouled andpolluted waters. The chronic condition of New York and San Francisco's bays, the Great Lakes and rivers throughout the country was catastrophic before FWPCA. Back then American interstate waters were predominantly neither drinkable, swimmable nor fishable.

Nevertheless government and congress could not remedy all deficiencies.It seems absurd, but whenever communities could not manage environmental problems, it required solutions on a federal level and whenever federal initiatives remained ineffective it became a community or state task once more.

[5] Karl Boyd Brooks, BEFORE EARTH DAY The Origins of American Environmental Law, 1945-1970 (University Press of Kansas, 2009), p. 186ff.
[6] Nelson, Beyond Earth Day: Fulfilling the Promise, p. 8
[7] Nelson, Beyond Earth Day: Fulfilling the Promise, p. 8ff.
[8] Boyd Brooks, BEFORE EARTH DAY, p. xi ff.
[9] Boyd Brooks, BEFORE EARTH DAY,p. xiii, 1.13f.
[10] Boyd Brooks, BEFORE EARTH DAY, p. 123

When New York City was hit by a serious smog incident in 1953, people living in other big cities became anxious. And so it happened that California issued a statewide comprehensive stationary regulatory system in 1959, which was followed by the first mobile source law one year later. These Californian initiatives set a new air quality standard and pressurized the federal government to take action as well.

In 1958 president Dwight D. Eisenhower called the first national "Conference on Air Pollution".To stress the problem of air pollution two Californian law professors, James Krier and Edmund Ursin, drafted *Pollution and Policy: A Case Essay on California and Federal Experience with Motor Vehicle Pollution, 1940-1975.*[11]

Inspired by the effects on human health of gaseous pollutants,Californian Senator Thomas Kuchel introduced bills to empower the US Department of Health and Human Services to prohibit the sale of motor vehicles that produced too many hydrocarbons.This short example shows that the State of California became a pacesetter in environmental law and so it stays in this position until today.

Though environmental laws had been passed before, their tendencies principally increased and took effect after the first Earth Day, but are legislations enough?In his book *Before Earth Day*, author Karl Boyd Brooks describes it like this: "Environmental law appeared steadily during a long, complicated process of legal change." He also says "environmental conditions [were] formed by centuries of ecological dynamics."[12]Werepeople perhaps too eager, were they expecting a quicker betterment of ecological conditions than time allowed?

Environmental law seemed exciting, even radical at the beginning of the 1970s, but it was often criticized that"state action tended to consist in curative rather than preventive measures".[13]

Many legal historians believe that the fundamental problem of the American citizen lies in the New Deal spirit.Many Americans believed that governmentwould solve any public issue, but the truth is that since the New Deal "a central problem of government lies in the vast area of administrative 'discretion' that often masks submission to the demands of powerful interest groups".[14] The problem is that government often negotiates about procedures, details and budgets, before it really brings something into action.Anyhow, people were highly optimistic after the first Earth Day; everyone thought that tomorrow could be saved easily. The fiery environmental movement evolved into a sort of cosmetic campaign. People cleared vistas and planted trees, littering fees were introduced,illuminated advertising was reduced, and state waters as well as the air appeared cleaner.[15] This odd form of environmentalism had the effect that pollution obvious to the eye was abolished, but not invisible dangers to human health and ecosystems such toxic chemicals or hazardous greenhouse gases. It seems that people did not want to be reminded of the awkward condition of the environment day by day. True to the motto: What the eye does not see, the heart does not grieve over. It is needless to mention that a mindset like this accumulates trouble, instead of solving problems.Although the 1970s are often called "the decade of the environment"politics remained business as usual and the public debate on environmental challenges often remained superficial.

In 1971 a so-called *Earth Tool Kit* was published by the organizers of the first Earth Day. It gave advice to citizens how to represent their environmental interests on a serious level.

The authors pointed out that a well-informed group of anxious citizens should rather consult a lawyer instead of just hoping for betterment. Yet this guide also criticized that citizens "often lose interest, even if they understand the technical issues".[16]

---

[11]Boyd Brooks, BEFORE EARTH DAY, p. 132 ff.
[12] Boyd Brooks, BEFORE EARTH DAY, p. 139, l. 32 ff.
[13] Boyd Brooks, BEFORE EARTH DAY, p. 133, l. 29 ff.
[14] Boyd Brooks, BEFORE EARTH DAY, p. 192, l. 19 ff.
[15] Robert C. Schultz, J. Donald Hughes, ECOLOGICAL CONSCIOUSNESS, p. vii
[16]Boyd Brooks, BEFORE EARTH DAY, p. 193, l. 28

The environmental movement was often suspended by far-right politics or the influence of Wise Use groups. Environmentalism even suffered an enormous backlash at the end of the 1970s and the beginning of the 1980s due to stagflation and the oil crisis of 1973.Nevertheless there is another reason why environmentalism did not evolve as promising as expected.

The acceptance of environmental law is widespread in the US, but few Americans are willing to mobilize against environmental pollution or to change their habits. This non-action is actually not to be underestimated; it even seems to be a core problem of the ecological crisis. Legal historian Karl Boyd Brooks warns: "Should this lassitude persist, environmental law's future will track labor law's past".[17]

Describing the current situation, environmentalist Neil Evernden goes the extra mile: "If there is one role that the original Earth Day continues to play, it is to show us that nothing has changed. Earth Day 1970 gives us a benchmark by which we can evaluate our "progress".[18]

2.3. Ecological Consciousness or Ecofascism?

If one had to time the environmental movement in the US, one would divide it into two waves of contemporary environmental concern. The first wave started by Earth Day I in 1970 and lasted until the time of economic stagflation (1979-1982). The second wave developed even stronger and halts from 1990 up to today.

Doubts about economic growth, pollution and technological progress grew when Ronald Reagan's administration tried to roll back the environmental progress systematically. Traditional conservation/environmental groups as the *Sierra Club*(1892) and newly established organizations like *Greenpeace* (1971) or *People for the Ethical Treatment of Animals/PETA* (1980) registered that more people than ever before applied for membership.At the time of the first Earth Day there was a clear difference between environmentalism and conservationism, but in 1984 public attention has drawn to global warming, so it happened that both movements started toset the same goals. The global character of the environmental crisis arranged it, so that contemporary environmentalist and traditional conservationist concerns became more fully integrated, at least since the beginning of the 1990s.[19]

There was always a spirit of optimism for the environmental movement, but speaking of waves shows that people's dedication fluctuates a lot. Many environmental amateurs have a fundamental misconception on ecology. They believe it was a kind of savior, a pure science that was able to tell us how to improve our environmental situation, whichteaches us how to do things. Actually this is not the concept of ecology, ecology was meant to describe the ecological situation and the conditions of ecosystems. Ecology simply analyzes, but does not find solutions. It can only help people to understand, but it will not change people's behavior inevitably.

This is a reason for environmental organizations to search for ways to broaden their political base, because good intentions are not enough.Another problem is that many ecological activists want to intervene in history, in order to bring a future advancement, instead of caring of today.Environmentalist Arne Naess labeled this attitude "shallow ecology", he wrote that "We don't need more abstract data about the "environmental crisis" and ever more powerful

---

[17]Boyd Brooks, BEFORE EARTH DAY, p. 208, l .42 f.

[18]Neil Evernden, "Ecology in Conservation and Conversation, " AFTER EARTH DAY: Continung the Conservation Effort, ed. Max Oelschlaeger (University of North Texas Press, 1992), p. 74, l .12 ff.

[19]Robert Paehlke, "Environmental Politics and Policy: The Second Wave, " AFTER EARTH DAY, p .3 ff.

technologies to fix the problems, but a sense of the living reality, the life-world in which we live."[20]

Many people rely on environmentalists solving all ecological problems sooner or later, because they are not willing to simplify their lives. Everybody needs to "think globally" and "act locally" to change something, but it would be absurd for anyone to think he or she can heal the planet on his or her own.[21] On the one hand the average western world citizen is well aware of the ecological crisis, but feigns ignorance. On the other hand some people seek for self-realization and identification through environmentalism, but this approach can lead to bio- and ecocentrism.

Feeling misunderstood and to assume that no one will understand the necessity of environmentalism can foster a new form of totalitarianism. Can deep ecology perhaps step by to a kind of ecofascism?

It is true that many environmental organizations do not feel the need to recruit members of other interest groups. Cooperation, for example with labor groups, seems to be seldom.

Instead of trying to find a common consent with others, environmentalists try to reach a wide audience by staying in their made nests. They expect others to approach them, whereas they could take a step forward, too. This intransigence makes it hardly surprising that environmentalists are sometimes rumored to be arrogant and to feel superior to others. This might be a popular misunderstanding, but it has to be corrected by taking action.

The environmental crisis is everybody's business that is why everybody needs to be incorporated; it makes certainly no sense to hide oneself away.

"No group has a monopoly interest over clean air or water"[22], but it is a troublesome fact that most environmentalists are whites belonging to the well-educated middle-class. Nevertheless, this does not mean minorities or the poor are less concerned, actually it is them who feel the impact of environmental pollution the most. It is "the black man living near an inner city truck route, and the Latino worker exposed to pesticides in the field who feel the sharpest bite of our disposable society."[23]

Anyhow it remains a fact that many people do not understand what Earth Day is really about. Once a year, companies buy into Earth Day and people pick up litter from the streets. To act this way is useless and both a sort of greenwashing, non better than the other. This behavior is reprehensible and for sure nobody will win a businessman over to environmentalism by simply talking to him, but in general an environmentalist will only change people's minds, if he talks to them, tries to understand them and shares experiences with them.

A public opinion poll concerning environmental progress, conducted by the *Gallup Organization* in 1999, found out that the majority of the Americans were satisfied with the environmental protection efforts of that decade. Many of them had the opinion that society, government and the public were highly concerned about that issue, but they also agreed that there was still room for improvement.[24]

This poll took place over ten years ago, but it shows us that plain recognition was still not enough.

---

[20] Dolores LaChapelle, "Deep Ecology and Nonhuman Others, " After Earth Day, p. 133, l. 19 ff.

[21] Michael E. Zimmerman, "THE FUTURE of ECOLOGY," After Earth Day, p. 177

[22] Nelson, Beyond Earth Day, p. 116, l. 34 f.

[23] Nelson, Beyond Earth Day, p. 116, l. 14 f.

[24] Nelson, Beyond Earth Day, p. 14

3. Cure for the Cancer or Cancer for the Cure?

In this section I will try to explain which role economy plays in the American society, as well as consumer behavior and the appreciation of technology and science. I will go into detail on how these involved parties interact, how much impact they have on the environmental progressand how far they influence the average American's behavior and thinking.

Beforehand, just in the sense of the American conspiracy tradition, the basic assumption might be: "If you want to save the planet. Trust no one!"

3.1. Big Business and Economic Growth

What is most important nowadays is to transform our Western world consumer societies into sustainable societies as fast as possible. Minerals and fossil fuels are non-renewable and limited, furthermore urban growth expedites this process. Particularly it can be said that *The Industrial Revolution* has brought influence on how we live and work today. In the 19th century animal labor has been replaced by cheaper fossil fuel energy step by step and our energy usage has increased ever since.

We use our cars on a daily basis regardless of the consequences, because mobility means a comfortable lifestyle and nobody is willing to abandon comfort. Mobility is still available and "availability [...] seem[s] to be worth the cost. As demonstrated in recent years, [the American] willingly go[es] to war to assure a continued supply of inexpensive energy."[25] The oil embargoes of 1974 and 1979 already showed how important energy conservation is, but it seems as if especially the American did not learn that easily, instead American roads are more frequented by gas-guzzling pick-ups and SUVs than ever before.

Natural resource problems are economic problems, which "result from the economic decisions of individuals"[26], blames E.E. Spitler. As a direct consequence hepredicts that it will be inevitable to raise gas prizes drastically.He also claims that gas and oil business is becoming less profitable in the present.Necessarily the industrial nations need to campaign for the development of alternative energies to a greater degree than they already do and above all American government will have to subsidize the expansion of public transport network in local communities.

In this development European cities will clearly serve as models, but it is not just European public transportation that is exemplary. Paris or Amsterdam for example are more compact cities than Los Angeles or Phoenix, as a resulttheir residents drive on average as half as many miles; but most likelyit will take a long time to transform American metropolitan regions this way, especially in the southwest.[27]

Nevertheless, history has taught us that whenever there was a lack of resources, people drew on new resources. The ancient Greeks switched from bronze to iron, and when the shortage of timber hit England in the 16th century, coal was discovered. Even the U.S. experienced their first energy crisis in the mid 19th century, whale oil was in short supply, but than petroleum was discovered.[28]

Due to a dire fallacy, embedded in people's minds, many believe that planet earth's resources are eternal, infinite, limitless and unchanging. Ancient rules defined nature as a resource; especially the American tradition views it as a national quest to own nature to accumulate wealth. The roots of those beliefs can be already found in Puritanism.

---

[25]E. E. Spitler, "The Energy Business and Conservation, " After Earth Day, p. 107, 1.14 f.
[26]Michael L. Nieswiadomy, "Economics and Resource Conservation, " After Earth Day, p. 120, l. 13 f.
[27]Paehlke, After Earth Day, p. 6
[28]Nieswiadomy, After Earth Day, p. 122

It will be very important for us "to define our environmental values primarily in relation to demands for steady economic growth"[29]. It is no wonder that economic growth has been increasingly criticized in recent years. Economic growth is not just harmful to the environment, it also leads to more social injustice. Economic growth does not eradicate poverty;it brings about an unfair distribution of its benefits. Economic growth symbolizes the American's absolute ideals, but it is no mandatory guaranty for liberty, freedom, opportunity, social stability and equality.

To avoid an anti-environmental political backlash in the future, it will be important to mobilize a "combination of environmental and (moderately) progressive politics"[30].

Earth Day and the environmental movement have been often called hostile to capitalism, economy and democracy, especially the costs of environmental protection have been feared a lot. A cost-benefit calculation of environmental progress is necessary and for sure the transformation of a consumer into a sustainable society will be expensive at the beginning. With regard to cost-benefit ratio, not everything that seems to be ecological is necessarily good for the environmental health. Recycling paper for example can save overcutting of limited forests, but deinking paper can turn into water pollution as well, due to usageof chemicals such as chlorine.

Despite all that, there is a "direct [...] connection between a healthy environment and a prosperous economy."[31]When nature is not able anymore to serve with resources like timber, water or minerals, economy goes into bankruptcy together with environment itself.

Consumer behavior is a very important factor of environmental pollution. National polls show that many American's are "sympathetic to environmental causes, but not active"[32]; the majority of them also have the opinion that the U.S. environment is getting worse.

57 percent of all "Americans said in 2001 that they would favor protecting the environment even at the risk of curbing economic growth."[33]The reality looks different:

Ecological consciousness is present, but it does not achieve much, because people do not behave conscious. Consumption did not alter, it even seems that Americans' craving for material goods grows. Statistics also report that convenience wins over ecology, because what matters in the end is the price. American people are not willing to buy eco-friendly, sustainable or organic productsthat are more expensive than others. *American Demographics* has even reported that fewer people inform themselves if a company is ecologically responsible, than did years ago. "It's as if many consumers take for granted that today's mainstream products treat the planet kindly."[34] It is also alarming that most Americans trust more in tests and researches commissioned by companies than in those commissioned by government or environmental organizations. For average Americans it is also hard to believe that most chemicals, pesticides and hormones used in agriculture have not yet been fully tested.In general the American sustainability movement is growing, but it is a very slowly advancing process. It is time for people to rethink their relation to corporations, economy and their disposable society.

Elliot Leyton's fact book*Dying Hard* from 1975 exemplifies very well the cost of profit and economic wealth. It shows what greed for money can mean for individuals and their families in specific. Leyton portrays the fates of Newfoundland miners working with toxic fluorspar, asbestos and lead. His book reports the miners' individual progress of disease,agonizing cases of death and how surviving dependants deal with it.[35]

---

[29]Leiss, Ecological Consciousness, p. 232, 1. 29ff.
[30]Paehlke, After Earth Day, p. 13, 1. 17f.
[31]Nelson, Beyond Earth Day, p. 18, 1. 30ff.
[32]Nelson, Beyond Earth Day, p. 106, 1. 4f.
[33]Nelson, Beyond Earth Day, p. 106, 1. 19ff.
[34]Nelson, Beyond Earth Day, p. 114, 1. 23f.
[35]Leiss, Ecological Consciousness, p. 218

Examples like this illustrate why many specialists demand stronger controls on enterprises since years, but the problem is that "market-based tools are traditionally advocated by the political right"[36]. Republicans are also proponents of cost and tax cuts, which makes them usually inhibit proposals on charges for domestic solid waste and individual metering of electricity and domestic water use, too.To us Europeans it might be a mystery that the American does not bear his individual energy costs, it may also sound like an abstruse argument to us that "raising the price of energy [...] hits the poor"[37].

The divide between rich and poor is evidently far smaller in Germany than in the U.S but per capita consumption of water in comparison, is lesser in Germany than in the United States. The average German's water use per person per day lies at less than 200 litres, but the American's water use is nearly 600 liters.[38] These basic statistics show that opposing the raise of energy prices needs a rethinking. Raising energy costs will ultimately make sure that the majority of the Americans will use water and electricity wiser.

Canada for example has shown that government can do its bit to demonstrate how to use energy and water more responsibly and how to behave more ecologically. Years ago the Canadian government had the key idea to bring together business circles, environmental and labor organizations and community groups to establish an ecological economy at government level. Many "state and local governments now purchase recycled paper and other environmentally advantageous products"[39]like organic food and cleaning supplies with fewer or no chemicals. They also invest into more energy saving vehicles and green buildings.

The only achievement in this direction that the U.S. government has made was the so-called CRC (Corporate Recycling Council). In 1989 the Texas General Land Office asked major companies with industrial premises in Dallas, such as Dr Pepper, Coca Cola, Mary Kay Cosmetics or the U.S. Postal Service to initiate a corporate recycling effort to reduce solid waste.[40]

To fully understand the dynamics of economy, it is necessary to also understand the environment and the consequences ofaware or unaware human intervention into ecosystems. It is not enough to know plain facts and statistics, knowledge has to be combined and converted into daily life. A new university subject could help to solve the environmental problem or at least help to answer more questions. An interdisciplinary subject combining ecology and economy could be guidelining and elementary in future.

3.2. Technology and Science, A Solution For All Problems?

There exists a certain misbelief in Western society: the belief that law and technology can correct everything. Industry appears to be the only chance for survival or improvement of life and for industry's sake;the risk of ecological destruction seems to be justifiable. Apparently we agree to pay this price, but we need to know thatthe value of a sound nature cannot be measured and no currency is strong enough to buy a new environment.

Technology and science are widespread forms of human intervention into nature, planned or capricious, they "pervert the flow of energy and the cycling of nutrients "[41] Chemical bioaccumulation in the food chain for example, is only one of many unpredictable effects.

---

[36]Paehlke, After Earth Day, p. 7, l. 11f.
[37]Paehlke, After Earth Day, p. 12, l. 15
[38]Data 360, *Average Water Use Per Person Per Day*,
http://www.data360.org/dsg.aspx?Data_Set_Group_Id=757 (September 2010)
[39]Paehlke, After Earth Day, p. 9, l. 16 ff.
[40]Jenny Cheek, "The Corporate Responsibility to the Environment," After Earth Day, p. 104
[41]Edward J. Kormondy, "HUMAN INTERVENTION INTO NATURAL ECOSYSTEMS: THE SCIENTIFIC BACKGROUND TO MORAL CHOICE, " Ecological Consciousness, p. 34, l. 18f.

An agricultural example for human intervention could be, that farmers have fed their swine with crops and leftovers in the past, today they are fed with factory-made food and due to a lack of nourishment they have to add protein supplements to the breeding cattle's diet.

So if one asked what humanity has brought to nature, the only possible reply would be civilization. Anyhow it is questionable, if self-centered human civilization is desirable for the environment. We actually observe that nature strikes back or at least suffers since the beginning of the 20th century. Natural disasters such as oil spills, floods, hurricanes, the disappearance of rainforests and the melting of arctic glaciers and ice caps are evidence enough.

Our blind faith in technology gets us into trouble, no matter if chemistry or biotechnology. There are many red flags scientists are raising, like the cumulative and synergistic effects of chemicals and pesticides reacting with one another. The potential for genetically modified crops to contaminate unmodified or even organic crops and the effects on other species.

It is a fact that scientific achievements influence life on earth, but as the invention of the atomic bomb, genetic engineering could have a disastrous effect, too.It is not surprising that growth based on industrial technology has often been seen as a failure. With this in mind it is incomprehensible that there are many "underrated externalities"[42]in understanding the dynamics of American society. For instance it is often ignored that the development and use of technologies shapes the American faith in democracy. Technology symbolizes standard of living and quality of life; consequently it forms public opinion and dominates policy.

Another key aspect of the American spirit is that the U.S. is a nation of optimists, where everything must be always on the go and whenever someone criticizes the system he is blamed of being pessimistic, although he is being realistic. Even objective well-documented scientific researches are considered as nay saying by the average American.

What physics and other natural sciences meant for people in the 17th century, new interdisciplinary sciences that go beyond plain ecologywould mean for us in the future.

Those new sciences will be required to reshape the human view on nature.

In his seminal book *Nature's Economy* Donald Worster points out that we all need to learn that a certain ontology exist in everyone of us, meaning that everybody is torn between ecology and economy.[43] Human beings create their own future, that is why progress of knowledge is crucial to scrutinize several mechanisms, but to refuse scientific and technological discovery completely would still be irrational.

As well as the Industrial Revolution, Marxist and liberal theories alike have contributed to the internalized image that "the future involves constant improvement in the human estate."[44] This ideal of progress grew stronger and stronger, but it leads to the naive optimism that the improvement of human life is inevitable. The attempt "to dominate nature [is bound to] backfire" and eventually "it might prove suicidal to our species"[45].

However, technology and science were meant to simplify daily life and to distribute wealth, always with demand for equality. Unfortunately the purpose of equality did not work out. Technology became a symbol for luxury and convenience. Many people in our Western society cannot afford these status symbols, never mind people in third world countries.

Some live in abundance and rest becomes more frustrated with each day.

This materialinjustice goes beyond plasma screens and SUVs; it increasingly becomes a big social problem. Overall science and technology are global issues that involve and influence environmental, social and economic fields.

---

[42]Leiss, Ecological Consciousness, p. 249
[43]Evernden, After Earth Day, p. 77
[44]Zimmerman, After Earth Day, p. 171, l. 19f.
[45]Zimmerman, After Earth Day, p. 171, l. 25ff.

4. The Third World and American Overpopulation

Alongside overconsumption, headless economy and other negative factors, overpopulation troubles the environment to a very heavy degree.

Many ecologists, sociologists and economists have tried to answer the question whether it is desirable to encourage our western lifestyle in the Third Worldor not, particularly with regard to restrain the growth of human populations. On the one hand overpopulation is a major issue in underdeveloped countries and it leads to an increase of the consumption of resources, but on the other hand our western lifestyle is the epitome of overconsumption. In this regard a western lifestyle would mean to adopt measures to reduce the birth rate in these countries. But is it ethical to expect other people to sacrifice their traditional lifestyle and their customs to accomplish this goal? Is it right to host infringements on personal liberties and properties for the purpose of an effective mandatory birth control? Chinas birth control politics for example or at least the consequence often appear brutal to us.

There is even one more moral conflict that emerges from the overpopulation issue. Experts claim that overpopulation and the associated lack of resources could limit options and liberties, as well as obligations to future generations. On the contrary opponents reproach that attributing rights to unborn or unspecifiable persons might result in absurdities.Whenever someone thinks of overpopulation, he immediately has underdeveloped countries in mind. Sure, Germany or Japan suffers from a declining birthrate the most, their population shrinks, while the population of countries such as India seems to explode, which is worrying.

At the United Nations International Conference on Population and Development in Cairo in 1994, 179 countries have signed a treaty that bounds them to stabilize their own population.[46] The U.S. has affirmed this agreement, too, but they did nothing to fulfill this obligation yet. The American populationpolicies, if maintained "will destroy the environmental achievements of recent years". Recent statistics predict that the U.S. population will double "to more than 500 million by around year 2075, and to around1 billion sometime in the next century."[47]It shows that overpopulation is not just a Third World problem; the U.S. will actually join India and China if they continue in the same style. Considering that the U.S. is the world's biggest CO_2 emitter after China, the American population issue appears even scarier, especially if one visualizes that more than 1.3 billion people inhabit China, but the U.S. only has 308 million citizens.[48]It soundsgloomy, but the U.S. could finally join less-industrialized nationsand become an underdeveloped country itself.

Right now the U.S. birthrate is about 2.1 children per woman on average, which is not too much, the average birthrate even seems to decrease from decade to decade.[49] What conduces the U.S. population growth is immigration, primarily legal immigration. The influx of immigrants leads to a yearly increase of population of about 1.3 million. To prevent further population growth it would be needful to set an immigration limit, "the number of legal immigrants entering" the U.S. "would have to match the number of emigrants leaving"[50], this would be about 220,000 annually.

Why did the U.S. governmentnot undertake action against that problem yet? The answer is simple though ridiculous. Many U.S. immigrants are of Hispanic descent, which makes nearly any discussion on population-immigration topics politically incorrect. Even the American

---

[46] Nelson, Beyond Earth Day, p. 134
[47]Nelson, Beyond Earth Day, p. 133, l .24f.
[48]Internationales Wirtschaftsforum Regenerative Energien, *Weltweiter CO2-Ausstoß*, http://www.iwr.de/klima/ausstoss_welt.html (September 2010)
[49]Nelson, Beyond Earth Day, p. 144
[50]Nelson, Beyond Earth Day, p. 144, l. 28f.

press is "frightened into silence by political correctness"[51], frightened to be charged with designations such as nativsm or racism.

The truth of the matter is that western nations will not solve other nations problems by just letting immigrants in. There lies a fundamental error in the system if people are not able to make their existence in their home country. It is also a fact that women in industrialized countries give less birth to children, first of all because they have access to education, jobs and family planning services, just to mention a few key aspects. It is assumable that these opportunities are lacking in overpopulated countries. According to this, wealthy nations should feel obliged to assist those countries and provide education, family planning, and economic and technical advice. Furthermore it should be our greatest concern to make other places in the world women friendly. It must no longer be possible to treat women like second-class citizens, as it is the case in India for example.

Besides we are not fully aware of the consequences of overpopulation. Civil wars for example are closely related to overpopulation. Ethnic or religious problems are often reasons that just follow the strain of overpopulation. Primarily conflicts arise from lack of space, nourishment and other resources. In this sense it is also very important to "recognize that the problems of poverty and underdevelopment cannot be solved unless we have a new era of" population and economic "growth in which developing countries play a large role and reap large benefits."[52]

Indonesia for example has often been pilloried for cutting down its rain forests, but Indonesia's economy is dependent on selling tropical timber to Europe and the U.S

One might even say that the maintenance of Indonesian rain forestsdepends on western consumer behavior. It shows that we have to overthink a lot of our fixed habits and that we have to give other countries the chance to solve themselves from their dependence on us.

5. Environmentally Friendly Behavior, a Question of Attitude?

Overconsumption, overpopulation etc. are these really the reasons for our ecologically harmful behavior or are these just symptoms of something else? It is clear that we need to switch our bad habits, but our consumer behavior has its reasons somewhere else. We behave the way we do, because there are certain values, ideals and ideologies deep-rooted in our minds. To reach our environmental goals we need to make profound thoughts and go below the surface. It will be unavoidable to search for deep solutions in human psychology, history, philosophy or even religion. Is it a matter of thinking or are we just puppets of primitive needs? Can we still learn something new?

5.1. A Matter of Religion and Philosophy

A general philosophical problem of our occidental culture has often been depicted as a major reason for our irresponsible dealing with the environment. So do we need a new philosophy? It is urgently required that we find a communication line between humanities and ecology, but is that possible when there exists human chauvinism? History simply seems to behuman centered from the scratch.

Actually naturalism "had its roots in the romantic transcendental movement."[53] So called naturalists only seemed to be fascinated by the beauty of nature and wild species, they did not

---

[51]Nelson, Beyond Earth Day, p. 145, l. 7f.
[52]Evernden, After Earth Day, p. 76, l. 13ff.
[53] Ralph H. Lutts, "THE NATURE FAKERS: CONFLICTING PERSPECTIVES OF NATURE, " Ecological Consciousness, p. 61, l. 40f.

make conservation their major concern. These nonrational, aesthetical and emotional motives were reasons for the "nature fakers controversy"at the beginning of the 20th century.

In 1967 Lynn White published a book named *The Historical Roots of Our Ecological Crisis* in which she argues that our fatal ecological attitudes were rooted in the Middle Ages.

Her theory lays the focus on theological and philosophical theses in specific. Christianity and Judaism in particular have taught us that mankind is the pride of divine creation, which apparently led humans to justify their attempt to subdue nature over centuries or at least it reinforced anthropocentrism. White also finds reasons in Greek philosophy; she claims that Socrates and other philosophers did not teach mankind that nature was an object of human responsibility.[54]

With this in mind, it is clear as crystal that it requires a new philosophy to change human thoughts, thus human behavior. Nonethelesswe need to be distinctly aware that a philosophy does not appear overnight, it must be deeply rooted. We live in an environmental state of emergency, i.e. we have to evaluate our traditional ways of living to adapt to the new circumstances of life. Human ecologist Joseph W. Meeker points out that it is necessary to shift our high humanistic goals. We will have to learn to fully respect the human species, but we will also have to recognize that we do not come first in the hierarchy of creatures.

We have to be willing to understand that all beings interact in various ways with each other and that every small part is a piece of the puzzle, regardless of whether plant, human, animal, water, soil or air.[55]

Philosophers have influenced history and society significantly, such as Hume, Locke, Smith or Marx, but currently only a few philosophers devote their work to ecological issues, in fact modern philosophy has to set a new trend on that score. Philosophers could make their contribution to change "the principles governing interhuman moral relationships."[56]

Generally people trust in expert knowledge that is why it is so important that philosophers talk to people, to share natural values and personal experiences with the environment. Unfortunately philosophers of science and philosophers of the humanities rarely or never cooperate. They "have made a traditional, if troublesome distinction between primary and secondary qualities."[57] It is beyond debate that both philosophicalfields have to approach, because to open up new perspectives different opinions have to be discussed, explained and understood. Otherwise there would be no room for successful solutions, if potential prejudices are not eliminated effectively.

Some ecologists claim that it is high time to adopt other philosophies, Calvin Martin for example has written the book *The American Indian as Miscast Ecologist*. It portrays the Indian as rolemodel for ecological consciousness, but other scholars see this point of view as a ridiculous and superficial caricature of the Native American. They also argue that the Native American could never function as a spiritual model for us, because our view on nature and our cultures were completely different.[58]Certainly it would be undesirable for us to live an oversimplified and primitive life in a wooden hut, but some Native American's daily techniques were superior to those of the settlers. For instanceminers have desertified Nevada by lumbering entire pinyon woodlands to make charcoal and this only within a few years,whereas the Nootka tribe had a highly sustainable method of cutting cedar wood. First of all they only cut trees which already had a notch caused by rocking winds, but they also did

---

[54]Kormondy, Ecological Consciousness, p. 47

[55]Joseph W. Meeker, "TOWARD A NEW NATURAL PHILOSOPHY, " Ecological Consciousness, p. 251ff.

[56] Ernest Partridege, "ENVIRONMENTAL ETHICS: OBSTACLES AND OPPORTUNITIES, " Ecological Consciousness, p. 326f.

[57]Holmes Rolston, "WHAT SORTS OF VALUES DOES NATURE HAVE?, " Ecological Consciousness, p. 352

[58]Schultz, Hughes, Ecological Consciousness, p. xiv

not cut the entire tree, only to the point of the half-section of the trunk. The effect was that the tree was still living; it could recover.[59]

Perhaps it is too late to learn from a declined culture, but we can try to sympathize with other modern cultures' views. "Amae" and "wabi" for example are special forms of Japanese ecological consciousness. The goal of these philosophies is to live a life oriented around simplicity,a selfhood rapt in nature and the understanding that human relationships depend on interplays between mankind and the environment.[60]

There are many sources of inspiration and many possibilities we could adopt to change our contemporary human ethics and ecological principles. Actually we have to get rid of the theory of a "global vision", in which planet earth is regarded as a human niche in which human beings rival every other living species. We also have to learn that we are not only responsible for our conscious actions, but that we are guilty of ignorance and indifference as well.[61]

Arne Naess, the founder of Deep Ecology, called for self-realization by trying to identify with all aspects of nature to achieve an inner and outer symbiosis with the whole environment.

To learn to "be like a tree"might sound like a very strange and abstract credo, but it is just a metaphor for a "new ecologically and psychologically sound way of living inharmony with our environment."[62]Nevertheless Deep Ecology should not turn into a totalitarian form of ecocentrism, but the ever-present anthropocentrism has to make way for real and new ideals of humanism.

5.2. Environmental Education

Environmental education is in a bad way all around the world, but how is it possible that there has been so little progress in environmental education in the U.S

U.S. Congress has already passed the National Environmental Education Act in 1970 under the Nixon administration, but it seems that the then republican government just wanted to calm the general public's concerns. The bill has sure been passed and placed within the EPA (Environmental Protection Agency), but little action was taken to definitely implement the Environmental Education Act.[63]

Unfortunately some big companies have in fact abused the issue of environmental education in the past. *Procter and Gamble*has distributed "educational packages " in more than seven thousand American schools. In their information booklets they claimed for example that clear-cut forestry would mimic natural processes. The *American Coal Foundation* even argued in an activity book for elementary schools that global warming made plants grow larger.The effect equipping children with sham knowledge was that kids became optimistic about the environmental situation, instead of fearful. As a consequence environmentalist groups and parental organizations cried havoc, but as a reaction the political right-wing promoted "that environmental education is taught with a one-sided, liberal bias."[64]

Luckily people like the political science professor Michael Sanera did fail miserably, although his book *Facts Not Fear: A Parent's Guide to Teaching Children about the Environment* from 1996 became a bible for the anti-environment movement. It is intolerable that a certain group of people surrounded by scientists and politicians tries to convince the American public that environmental problems do not exist.Legislation and education are the pillars of the

[59]LaChapelle, After Earth Day, p. 137
[60]Schultz, Hughes, Ecological Consciousness, p. xvi
[61]Evernden, After Earth Day, p. 78
[62]Lutts, Ecological Consciousness, p. 203, l. 7ff.
[63]Nelson, Beyond Earth Day, p. 147f.
[64] Nelson, Beyond Earth Day, p. 122, l. 31f.

environmental effort, but if the discourse on environmental education will not be initiated now, "it will delay by years and years"[65]. U.S. Government and the American public still do not see the link between environmental education and a sustainable economy. People also discount that environmental education could get society and policy to debate and learn about environmental issues. If people's attitude would change at least a little bit, media and journalism would feature environmental problems more, the environment could finally become a daily and self-evident issue. We should be conscious that media usually informs us on topics that are important for us.

Environmental law and other academic fields such as environmental history or ecology may help to find more insights which can prove advantageous for the whole society, but in general specific knowledge remains an elitist privilege. That is why environmentally relevant knowledge has to become accessible for everyone, because everybody is involved in environmental nuisances; consequently everybody needs to know important matters of fact.

In all objectivity it will be a formidable challenge to convince adults to change their already learned habits. Socially and psychologically speaking, behavior modification for adults needs really tough measures. To prevent the same mistakes in future generations we need to teach children a completely new way of behavior and habits, but it will not work as effectively as required if environmental education starts about the age of ten. Children have to be introduced to a healthy environmental approach as early as toddler age, because the more playful the way of learning is shaped at the beginning, the bigger is the chance to found a deeply rooted basic understanding of human interaction with nature and human responsibility for the environment.

It is inevitable to teach children the value of an intact nature, if we want to make the step into a sustainable society. "Many solutions require a change in behavior, and often denial is the easiest path."[66] Another positive effect of environmental education might be that it can connect communities and families. Families can take part in state environmental department or state park education programs to learn something about their local environment, which makes environmentalism even more concrete.[67]

Anyhow, it seems to be prestigious and desirable to create and establish an efficient environmental education for children and adolescents, but how can this endeavor be achieved? Many young American students are not as eager to make a Wallstreet career as students have been about thirty years ago, au contraire they pursue to save the planet, but do they suffer from megalomania as a consequence of which? The answer is No, because they want to save the planet all together.It will be the youth again, the next generationwho will have to change and achieve something for the environment like back in the days of 1970.

6. Conclusion

It is absolutely certain that the first Earth Day in 1970 has raised environmental concern, mobilized the American public and inspired other nations. The environmental movement of the 1970s has initially experienced aeuphoric enthusiasm, but this excitement faded after a while, which turned out to be somewhat disappointing. Notwithstanding, Earth Day helped to convert environmentalism from an allegedly radical element of the hippie culture into a socially acceptable issue. Even if environmental law had its very existence long before Earth Day, it was still in the early stages of development back then. Environmental law did not outgrow itself before 1970. It is due to politicians like Gaylord Nelson that environmentalistsand legislation could find a common platform.

---

[65]Nelson, Beyond Earth Day, p. 139, l. 19f.
[66]Nelson, Beyond Earth Day, p. 134, l. 30f.
[67]Nelson, Beyond Earth Day, p. 150

No one could claim that Earth Day has failed. The Earth Day movement has achieved a lot to a certain level, such as the improvement of air and water quality on U.S. territory and more consumer protection.Still the environmental movement was not according to expectations, because most Americans leaned back on environmental activism.They thought the others would do the job, they neither scrutinized their own habits nor did they question how they could make a contribution towards the environmental effort. No other nation wastes energy and resources so unscrupulously as the United States of America. The ongoing American ecological crisis is caused by mindless consumer behavior and lobbyism. Although western lifestyle is questionable in general, in comparison to Europeans, Americans top the bill.

A city like Las Vegas, Nevada, devouring money, electricity, water and gas is a symbol for capitalistic throwaway insanity. The American saying, "What happens in Vegas, stays in Vegas!" might be true in a moral sense, but this city leaves a giant carbon footprint.

Las Vegas as an example of Americanismmight be an exaggerated generalization, but in fact the American citizen will have to overthink and overcome his habits of consumption. Environmental consciousness and responsibility are highly linked to a healthy economy; each individual will have to recognize it, better sooner than later.

It is shocking that the average American consumer seems either to trust companies like *Nutra Sweet* blindly or sees himself as a victim, but only few question their individual economic choices.Convenience food for example can threaten health, as well as overconsumption of meat, besides that keeping of farm animals is the largest causer of CO_2 emissions. This does not mean that everybody should become vegetarian or vegan, but reducing animal source food on a daily basis would be reasonable for various reasons. It should be obvious that the reasons for environmental problems also involve other risks, but apparently it is not, at least for the majority.

Global warming and all its causes and consequences pose the greatest problem of the present, because sick ecosystems lead to a sick society by detours. Regaining a healthy environment will be a challenge, which is why we have to start to think of precaution, not just aftercare. We need a new philosophy that is built around the credo of respect for Mother Natureto achieve new social structures. Anthropocentrism is bound to fail, so it has to come to an end before it reaches a "greater" apocalyptical dimension.Most of all, it is all about education, philosophy and cooperation between environmentalists, scholars, economists, industrialists, politicians, media, public and all social classes, these different factors are infiniteon the way to save the environment.The environmental situation has to be an appeal for the American right-wing in specific. Conservatives have to become insightful, they have to understand that environmentalism is not socialistic or harmful, on the contrary it is essential for America's and the world's future.Alas it seems too naive to believe or hope that they could shift their ground soon.Last but not least, performing Earth Day once a year just to silence the conscience is pointless. People should try act eco-friendly every day, to "make every day Earth Day."Earth Day is still in process and the youngest generation will play the largest role to fulfill the promise of Earth Day.

7. Pictorial Sources

-Picture 1: front page[68]

-Picture 2: The November 1969 issue of the Gaylord Nelson from his Senate office.[69]

THE GAYLORD NELSON NEWSLETTER

Washington, D.C.

November 1969

Environmental Teach-In Planned

National Effort Set For Spring

The development of comprehensive plans to kick off a national teach-in on the Crisis of the Environment to take place this spring on college campuses across the country will be announced this month by Sen. Gaylord Nelson.

The Wisconsin senator said he has been traveling around the country talking about his teach-in idea and seeking support for the proposal.

By the end of the month, Nelson expects to have a national headquarters on the teach-in set up in Washington with a staff that will be contacting students all across the country.

The teach-in plans call for a day, probably in April, when normal campus activities will be set aside for the university and the local community to get together and discuss the mutually shared environmental problems.

Discussions, Rallies

On that day, special programs designed and planned by the students will take the form of symposiums, convocations, panel discussions or outdoor rallies where the crisis of the environment will be discussed.

Nelson said the topics of discussion will vary with the university and the section of the country in which it is located. For example, students at the University of California might want to discuss oil spills in the ocean, while students at the University of Wisconsin might want to talk about the pollution crisis in the Great Lakes. At Columbia University the subject might be air pollution of American cities.

"The initial reaction to the teach-in idea has been impressive and

Apostle Islands Legislation

The Nelson bill to establish Apostle Islands as a part of the national park system passed the Senate in June, and the Senator is hopeful the House will authorize the necessary money to make the proposal a reality by the end of next year.

beyond what I had hoped," Nelson said. "My office has been receiving mail from students and people from all parts of the nation wanting to know how to become involved and how to plan a teach-in."

The Washington office will be filtering the mail and offering whatever support the various colleges are requesting.

Student Commitment

Nelson said he decided on a teach-in for college students because the present national commitment toward environmental problems indicates it may be too late to convince the established leadership of the serious ness of the crisis.

"This generation of youth is vitally concerned about the environment, because it will inherit the

disaster of years of wanton, indifference and waste and destruction of the natural resources of the country," Nelson argued. "If something isn't done soon, there may be nothing left for their children."

The senator believes that the same concern the youth of the nation took in changing the country's attitude on the war in Vietnam and on civil rights can be shown for the problems of the environment.

"What is heartening," Nelson continued, "is that modern youth is not satisfied with coming out the loser in man's drive for progress and profit. Because of the indifference of their elders, the young people of today face an ugly world of the near future with dangerously bad deadly polluted air and water, sprawling, crowded development, festering mounds of debris, and an insufficient amount of open space to get away from it all."

Quality Of Life

He said he is hopeful that the climax of the teach-in will be a demand for a quality of life in the final third of the 20th Century "that gives the same priority and money to the crisis facing the environment as has been given to national defense."

Nelson added that "it will take the same kind of commitment that put men on the moon and built one of the most massive defense machines ever seen on earth to solve the environmental crisis."

Environmental Guinea Pigs

"WE DON'T REALLY KNOW WHAT THE LONG-TERM EFFECTS OF VARIOUS TYPES OF ENVIRONMENTAL DETERIORATION WILL BE, AND THE KIDS ARE THE GUINEA PIGS."

Barry Commoner
Biologist
Chairman, St. Louis Committee for Environmental Information

---

[68]Caldwell College, *EARTH DAY REFLECTION 2009 "OUR CARBON FOOTPRINT"*, http://www.caldwell.edu/news/earth_day_2009.aspx (October 2010)

[69]Board of Regents of the University of Wisconsin System Nelson Institute for Environmental Studies, *A proposal reprinted across the country*, http://www.nelsonearthday.net/earth-day/proposal.htm (September 2010)

-Picture 3: Gaylord Nelson speaks to an Earth Day crowd in Denver, Colorado, on April 22, 1970.[70]

-Picture 4: students celebrate Earth Day in Manila in front of a "tree of knowledge"[71]

---

[70]Board of Regents of the University of Wisconsin System Nelson Institute for Environmental Studies, *April 22, 1970*, http://www.nelsonearthday.net/earth-day/4-22-1970.htm (September 2010)
[71]Axel Springer AG 2010/ WELT ONLINE, *Ein "Tag der Erde" für die Umwelt 11 von 12*, http://www.welt.de/wissenschaft/article3601135/Ein-Tag-der-Erde-fuer-die-Umwelt.html (July 2010)

-Picture 5: World Population Growth[72]

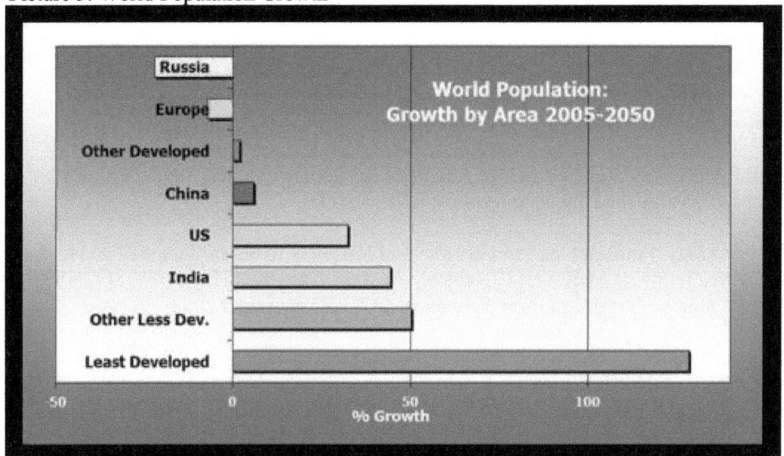

-Picture 6: Average Water Use[73]

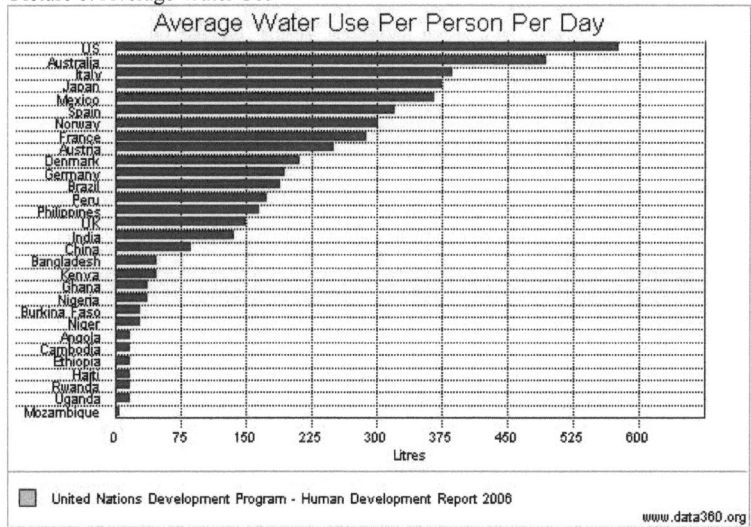

[72]Salon Media Group, Karl's Blog, *Global Warming 5:Just Too Many Of You*,
http://open.salon.com/blog/karll/2007/03/14/global_warming_5_just_too_many_of_you (September 2010)
[73]Data 360, *Data Graphs*, http://www.data360.org/dsg.aspx?Data_Set_Group_Id=757 (September 2010)

8. Bibliography

Literature:

-AFTER EARTH DAY: Continuing the Conservation Effort; Max Oelschlaeger, Editor//
University of North Texas Press; First Edition 1992

-BEFORE EARTH DAY The Origins of American Environmental Law, 1945-1970; Karl
Boyd Brooks; 2009 by the University Press of Kansas 1st Edition

-Beyond Earth Day, Fulfilling the Promise; Gaylord Nelson with Susan Campbell and Paul
Wozniak with a foreword by Robert F. Kennedy Jr.; THE UNIVERSITY OF WISCONSIN
PRESS 1930 Monroe Street, Madison, Wisconsin 53711; Copyright© 2002

-ECOLOGICAL CONSCIOUSNESS: Essays from the Earthday X Colloquium, University of
Denver, April 21-24, 1980; Edited by Robert C. Schultz, J. Donald Hughes; [Copyright©
1981 by University Press of America, Inc.™ P.O. Box 19101, Washington, DC 20036]

Online Sources:

- Board of Regents of the University of Wisconsin System Nelson Institute for Environmental
Studies, *Gaylord Nelson and Earth Day, the making of the modern environmental movement*,
http://www.nelsonearthday.net/index.htm (September 2010)

-Data 360, http://www.data360.org/index.aspx (September 2010)

- IWR®, *Die Business-Welt der Regenerativen Energiewirtschaft*, http://www.iwr.de/
(September 2010)

- © 2010 Salon Media Group, Inc*Karl's BlogHumanistic Liberalistic Artistics*,
http://open.salon.com/blog/karll/2007/03/14/global_warming_5_just_too_many_of_you
(September 2010)

- © Axel Springer AG 2010 WELT ONLINE, *Wissenschaft, Alles über die Welt des Wissens*,
http://www.welt.de/wissenschaft/ (September 2010)